Events of the Revolution

Yorktown

By Susan and John Lee

Illustrated by Michael Norman

CHILDRENS PRESS, CHICAGO

GLOUCESTER
POINT

YORK
RIVER

N

W

SIEGE OF YORKTOWN
BEGINS SEPT. 29, 1781

E

YORKTOWN

BOMBARDMENT
BEGINS OCT. 9, 1781

S

CORNWALLIS
SURRENDERS
OCT. 19, 1781

MOORE'S HOUSE
WHERE ARTICLES
OF CAPITULATION
WERE SIGNED OCT. 19, 1781

Library of Congress Cataloging in Publication Data

Lee, Susan.
    Yorktown.

    (Events of the Revolution)
    SUMMARY: Chronicles the execution of Washington's
plan that trapped Cornwallis at Yorktown and won the
Revolution for the Americans.
    1. Yorktown, Va.—Siege, 1781—Juvenile literature.
|1. Yorktown, Va.—Siege, 1781. 2. United States—
History—Revolution, 1775-1783| I. Lee, John, joint
author. II. Norman, Michael. III. Title.
E241.Y6L43   975.5'423   75-9598
ISBN 0-516-04677-2

Up to Yorktown . . .

The Americans and English had been at war since 1775. The fighting had begun in New England. Lexington, Concord, Breed's Hill, and Boston had seen fighting. In March, 1776, the English had left Boston.

The war blew wide open in the Middle Colonies during 1776 and 1777. The English captured New York City and held it. An English army from Canada pushed down into New York. It was beaten badly and 5,700 English soldiers were captured. The English captured Philadelphia, but moved out and marched back to New York City.

The English then moved to the Southern Colonies. In 1778, Savannah, Georgia, fell to the English. Charles Town, South Carolina, was captured in 1780. During 1780 and 1781, the war was fought in the Carolinas. At last the English moved into Virginia and dug in at Yorktown. In September, 1781, the French navy beat the English navy off Virginia. Now, it was the English army that was in trouble.

Chapter 1
THE HANGING ROPE

August, 1781

The Americans were strung out along the New Jersey shore. They were soldiers, but they weren't fighting. They were building ovens. Day after day they had made bricks from clay. Day after day they used the bricks to build ovens.

"This is a fool way to fight a war," said Robert Pincus Potts. "I'm a gunner, right? I fire cannon, right? Then General Knox sends me down here. But all I do here is make bricks and build ovens."

The quiet soldier working with Potts didn't say a word. He knew Potts could talk a streak.

"And look where we're building the dumb ovens. Right on the dumb New Jersey shore. Those English across the Hudson can see us."

Potts stopped and picked skin off his sunburned nose. "What are ovens for? To bake bread in! That's what! What are 1,000 ovens for? To bake 10,000 loaves of bread, that's what! Who's going to eat all those loaves of bread? An army, that's who. Don't you agree? Sure you do."

The quiet soldier went on piling bricks. Potts let his burned nose alone and pointed across the river. "What about old General Clinton over there in New York City? Don't you think he knows about ovens and bread? About bread and soldiers? Of course he knows."

The quiet soldier took a drink of water.

"What's wrong with General Washington?" asked Potts. "This isn't any way to attack a city. I think we need a new general. I think we need a general who doesn't let the English in on his plans."

The Americans went on building ovens until the third week in August. Then their officers led them to Princeton. From Princeton they marched to Trenton. At Trenton, the men camped for two days.

Robert Pincus Potts watched the American army march through Princeton. "Six hours," he said, "they been marching past us for six hours. Most of them are New England men. Some are New York or New Jersey troops. Fat General Knox went past with more cannon than I knew we had. I saw my own battery of cannon roll by. Washington must have the whole army on the march."

"Funny way to get to New York, ain't it?" asked the quiet soldier. "You did say our dumb general was going to attack New York City?"

"I said it, but now I take it back," said Potts. "I was wrong, but . . . Hold it! Look at that cavalry! You ever see them before?"

"Blue coats and yellow pants," said the quiet one, "black hats and white feathers. No, I never saw any cavalry dressed like that."

"The officers, look at the officers!" shouted Potts. "Red pants and tiger-skin saddlecloths. By George! They're French! The French are here with Washington. The French are helping us!"

"Here come the foot soldiers. All in white.
They must be French, too."

"I don't get it," said Potts, "where are they
going?"

They were going to Philadelphia. From there
the army marched into Delaware. They crossed
into Maryland. They stopped at the water known
as the Head of Elk. There the army climbed
into boats, ships, and barges.

Potts and the oven-builders had marched at
the end of the army. "Now I get it," said Potts,
"we're going to Virginia. From here we go

down Chesapeake Bay. Then we go up the James River. General Wayne and General Lafayette are down there somewhere."

"If we're going to Virginia," asked another soldier, "what were all those bake ovens for?"

"That's easy, they were a trick." said Potts. "Washington wanted the English to think he was going to attack New York. Clinton thinks *he's* going to be attacked, so he keeps all his soldiers in New York. He's afraid to send help to his army in Virginia. Washington tricked him!"

"Won't Clinton send help to Virginia now?"

"Ain't you heard?" asked Potts. "The French navy beat the English navy. The French navy can keep the English help out of Virginia."

The Americans and French did move down Chesapeake Bay and up the James. They joined Lafayette and Wayne near Williamsburg. More and more soldiers came into camp. At last Washington had about 16,000 soldiers.

On September 14, Washington rode through his camps. The Americans cheered as he rode past them. The French held their muskets high and shouted, "Vasinton!" They shouted, "Rochambeau" for their own general who rode beside "Vasinton."

Potts walked up to the quiet soldier and shook his hand. "Time to say good-bye," he said. "I'm being sent back to my battery. You know, this army is like a rope. A rope for hanging an English army."

Chapter 2
THE LOOSE NOOSE

September 28-October 9

Robert Pincus Potts was back with his New York battery of cannon. His old friends were glad to see him.

"Hey, old boy," said Dutch VanTen, "come sit by the fire. Where you been? What you been doing? You miss us New York boys?"

"Sure did," said Potts. He put his finger to his lips. "But what I've been doing is a secret. Can you keep a secret? I been with General Washington. He needed some help on how to win this war. He wanted me to help him out. Yes sir, the general gave me a horse and let me ride along with him."

Dutch grinned and said, "Potts, you always could tell a tall tale. Sounds like you still can. So, you rode one of General Washington's horses? The closest you got to the general's horse was its tail. You were walking behind it with a broom and shovel."

Captain Lamb walked up and kicked the wood out of the fire. "On your feet," he ordered. "We're moving out. Hello, Potts, good to have you back. I bet you've told a tall tale a minute since you got back."

The men laughed at Potts as they hitched up the horses to the cannon. They were still laughing as they loaded gunpowder into wagons.

"Roll out!" ordered Captain Lamb. "And look like soldiers! Old Von Steuben is up ahead. He'll be swearing if we don't look smart."

The cannon pulled out into the road. Every man did his job. Every man looked like a perfect soldier. General Von Steuben, a German, had trained most of them. At Valley Forge he had turned them from raw boys into trained soldiers. They wanted to look good in front of him. They did.

Before long the cannon were led off the road. The men began to dig pits for the cannon. They piled the 16-pound cannonballs next to the cannon. They dug deep pits for the gunpowder.

General Lafayette rode up and began talking to Captain Lamb. Potts and Dutch tried to hear what they were saying.

". . . Virginians under Febiger in front of you . . . Wayne's Pennsylvania boys to the right . . . New Yorkers under Alexander Hamilton behind you . . . we are about a mile from the English . . . tomorrow . . . out to our right . . . cross Wormeley's Creek . . . River York." General Lafayette turned his horse and rode off.

Captain Lamb looked at Potts and Dutch. "Don't dig too deep," he said. "We won't be here long."

The Americans moved out to their right the next day. They crossed Wormeley's Creek and pushed up close to the English outer line. General Lincoln camped near the Moore house down by the York River.

Now the French, under Rochambeau, and the Americans, under Lincoln, were in place. Their lines curved for six miles around Yorktown. The French line ran from the York River to Beaverdam Creek. The American line ran from Beaverdam Creek to Wormeley's Creek and the York River. The English in Yorktown had these two armies in front of them. Behind them was the York River.

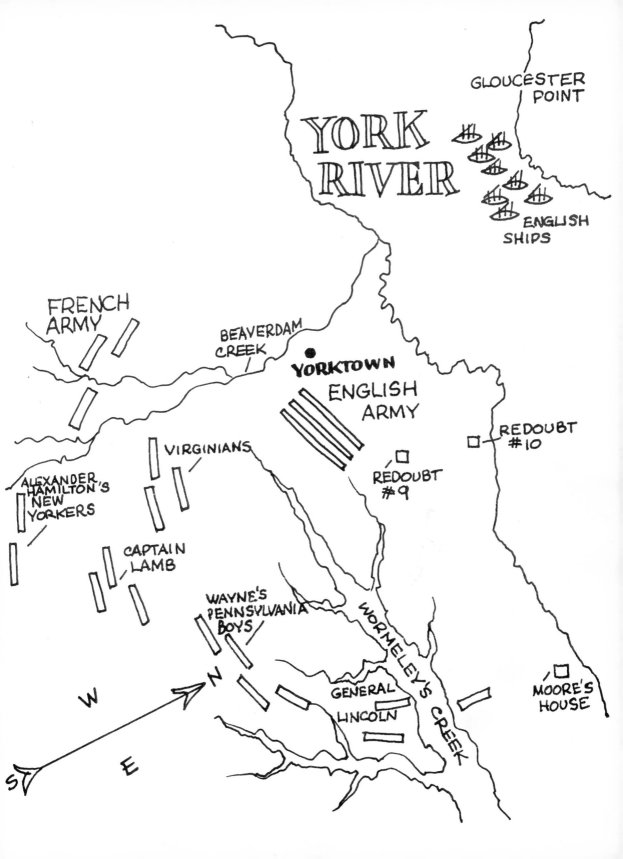

The French made a great discovery on the morning of September 30. The English had pulled back their outer line during the night. The Americans sent their scouts out. The English in front of them had also pulled back.

The French and Americans moved into the empty English lines. They began to dig trenches (long, deep ditches). The English cannon began to fire at them. At the end of four days the digging was over. The trenches were done. A rope of soldiers was now thrown loosely around the English.

Robert Pincus Potts asked if he could use Captain Lamb's spyglass. Lamb gave him the spyglass. Potts and Dutch climbed a small hill and looked at Yorktown.

"Two English ships out there in the river," said Potts. "The one on the right is the *Charon*. The other one must be the *Guadaloupe*."

"Can we hit them with our cannon?" asked Dutch.

"Not unless we move our cannon closer to Yorktown," said Potts. "We'd have to get about halfway between where our front lines and their front lines are now."

"Then we can bet our soldiers will move up again soon," said Dutch. "If we could get 1,000 yards from Yorktown, we could hit those ships."

On the night of October 6, the French attacked west of Yorktown. They fired their muskets and then fell back. It was another of Washington's tricks. The English were watching the French. About 4,300 Americans slipped out between the lines. Over 1,500 of them started digging. The other 2,800 guarded the diggers.

"Dig, dig, dig," said Potts. "All we do is dig. I used to be a fat man. Now I'm just a thin digger."

"Dig," said Captain Lamb. "If this trench isn't deep enough by morning, the English will blow our heads off."

By morning the trench was 2,000 yards long. It was about 800 yards from the English lines. The Americans had the right side. The French had the left. Both went on digging for two more days.

"Dig, dig, dig," said Potts. "If we dig much more, there won't be enough of me to throw a shadow."

"Look at it this way," said Captain Lamb, "you're learning a trade. When you get back to New York City, you can always get a job."

Potts snorted, "Learning a trade! You think I want to dig holes all my life. Not me. I want a nice quiet job. Something like pushing a pen. Or turning pages in a book."

"Right now," said Lamb, "you men can push this cannon into place. Get it up there."

The men shoved and pushed. They got their cannon into place. Potts looked down the long barrel of his cannon. "Well, well," he said, "hello there, Yorktown."

Chapter 3
THE TIGHT NOOSE

October 9 - 13

BOOM! BOOM! BOOM!

Robert Pincus Potts looked up. "That's the French cannon up on the other side of Yorktown. Goldang! When are *we* going to fire our cannon?"

Captain Lamb patted the cannon Potts and Dutch worked with. "Load it and aim it," he said.

The soldiers in the trench became very quiet. General Washington came down the trench. He walked up to Captain Lamb. The captain said, "We are pleased you will fire the first American cannon."

Captain Lamb led Washington to Potts' cannon. BOOM! the cannon fired and the men cheered. Washington left and Captain Lamb looked at Potts. "That was real, but it will sound like one of your tall tales."

The men all laughed. Dutch said, "Yah, no one will believe Potts when he tells this story. But my grandchildren, they will believe me."

"You ain't even married," said Potts.

"I will be," said Dutch. "After this war ends. Then you watch the children come. Then they will have their children. I will be an old man sitting by the fire. I will tell them this story."

"Goldang," said Potts, "so will I!"

"Yah," said Dutch, "but people will believe me."

Captain Lamb was looking at Yorktown with his spyglass. The French cannon had driven the *Guadaloupe* off. The English had sailed over to Gloucester Point. "Keep firing at the English lines," he said. "That other ship is too far away for us to hit it."

On October 10, the Americans and French
had 52 cannon firing. The French hit the
Charon with red-hot cannonballs. The *Charon*
burned and sank.

The 52 cannon kept firing. One by one the
English cannon were hit. The English began to
pull the rest of their cannon into deep holes.
Their lines were quiet. The American cannon
roared and roared and roared.

"Goldang, I never heard anything like this," said Potts.

"What?" yelled Dutch. "I can't hear you."

"Keep firing," yelled Captain Lamb. "Hit those English trenches. Make those redcoats keep their heads down."

"Keep their heads down?" said Potts. "Our good generals must want us to move up again soon."

"What?" yelled Dutch. "I can't hear you."

That night the Americans and French moved out again. This time they moved to within 300 yards of the English. They dug all night. They dug trenches for three more days.

Captain Lamb looked through his spyglass. He said, "We're closer to the English now, so our new trenches are shorter. They start at the York River. Then they curve around to that high ground in front of the French."

"What about that high ground, Captain?" asked Potts. "Will they dig trenches in front of that?"

"They won't have to," said Captain Lamb. He bent down and drew a map in the dirt. "Here's the river . . . Yorktown . . . the high ground. Here's Yorktown Creek in front of the high ground. The creek is in a deep ditch. If the English try to break out there, we've got them. If they get into that ditch, our cannon can blow them to bits. They wouldn't have a chance."

Potts poked at the right end of the dirt map. "Then our soldiers will attack here," he said. "We'll hit the east end of Yorktown."

"I think you are right," said Captain Lamb. "But there are two problems. There are two redoubts—strong dirt forts—we will have to take. One is here by the river road. It's called number 10. Number 9 is here by the other road into Yorktown."

"Those redoubts aren't going to be easy to take," said Potts.

Just then an officer came along the trench. He gave a note to Captain Lamb. Captain Lamb read it and nodded. The officer left. The captain walked over to Potts and Dutch.

"You two are going for a walk," Lamb said. "You are to work your way along this trench. When you get to the river road, you follow it up to our new trench. Then find Colonel Hamilton."

Colonel Alexander Hamilton of New York?" asked Potts.

"Yes," said Captain Lamb.

"Good," said Dutch. "We know him when we see him."

"What's he want with us?" asked Potts.

"I don't know," said Lamb, "but he asked for two of my best cannon gunners."

Chapter 4
THE CHOKING KNOT

October 14 - 17

Robert Pincus Potts and Dutch VanTen
found the place where the river road crossed the
trench. They started to climb out.

"Hold it!" shouted a captain. "Where the
blazes do you think you're going?"

"Up to the new trench, sir," said Potts. "We
have to find Colonel Hamilton."

"All right," said the captain. He pointed,
"The road forks right out there. You take the
right fork. Keep to the bushes beside the road.
You should make it if you keep in the bushes."

Potts and Dutch slipped out of the trench.
They ran for the right fork of the road. They

got into the bushes. Potts could feel his heart hammering inside his chest. He looked at Dutch and knew he was scared, too.

"Goldang," said Potts, "you see anyone out here?"

"No, I don't see anyone," said Dutch.

"Stop shaking the bushes," said Potts.

Dutch laughed and held up both hands. "That's not me. You're the one holding on to the bushes."

"It just seems like every redcoat can see us out here. I wonder what Hamilton wants with us?"

"Maybe he heard how good you rode one of General Washington's horses," said Dutch. "Maybe he wants you to tell him how to ride a general's horse."

"Shut up," said Potts. "Let's get moving."

"You lead," said Dutch. "I'll be right behind you."

The two men walked carefully until they were in a little valley. They knew the English

couldn't see into the valley, so they sat and
rested. They could see the York River on their
right.

Off they went again. They moved up a low hill
and got into the bushes again. The road forked
so they stayed to the right. Soon they could see
the red dirt behind the American trenches.
They ran the last 100 yards. Running seemed
safer than walking.

They jumped over the pile of dirt and slid into
the trench. They both sat, puffing and panting

like hunting dogs. There were many New York soldiers in the trench. Some were watching the English lines. Most were resting.

"Anyone know where Colonel Hamilton is?" asked Potts.

"Go up to your left," said a soldier. "He's up there talking to the French."

Potts and Dutch worked their way up the trench. They kept asking for Colonel Hamilton. The soldiers kept pointing toward the French end of the trench.

When they saw the colonel, he was talking to a French officer. Potts and Dutch waited. An American captain walked over to them. He asked if they were the gunners.

"Yes sir," said Potts. "We were sent down to see the colonel."

"I'm Captain Wolfe. Colonel Hamilton and the French colonel are cooking up something."

"For us or for the English?" asked Potts.

"For the English, smartmouth," said Captain Wolfe. "The colonel has already cooked up something for you."

At last Colonel Hamilton started back down the trench. He waved for Potts and Dutch to follow him. Captain Wolfe walked behind the gunners.

Colonel Hamilton stopped. He and Wolfe looked out at the English trenches. First one and then the other would point at something and talk.

Dutch said, "I think they're talking about that redoubt."

Potts nodded, "Yeh, that's number 10. Someone is going to be going out there. I got a feeling *we* are going out there."

"Why?" asked Dutch. "We're gunners. What do we know about bayonet fighting? It'll take bayonet fighting to win that place."

Captain Wolfe waved to Potts and Dutch. He pointed at redoubt number 10. He told them 400 Americans would attack it that night. He said the French would attack number 9 at the same time. He said he thought there were 70 or 75 English in each redoubt. He told them they were going along on the attack.

Potts and Dutch ate supper. They cleaned their muskets. They sharpened their bayonets. Captain Wolfe came by again. "You're not in the first group," he said. "You've got a special job. We'll take the redoubt. Your job is see if we can set up cannon in it. Is that clear?"

Potts and Dutch said it was clear. They were glad they weren't in the first group. Potts said, "Looks like we traded a Lamb for a Wolfe."

"Yah," said Dutch, "but Wolfe isn't so bad. He wants us to get there alive. We won't be much good to him dead."

WHOOOSH! . . . the rocket shot into the air. SPLAT! . . . its little stars spread out in the sky. Colonel Hamilton led his men out of the trench. Down to the left, the French colonel led out his men.

Potts and Dutch followed the New Yorkers. They were on their way to knot a rope under the chins of the English army. It was to be a choking knot.

Chapter 5
WORLD UPSIDE DOWN

October 17 - 19

It took Hamilton's men 10 minutes to capture number 10. There had been about 70 English in it. The English had fought bravely. There had been little shooting but much bayonet work.

It took the French 30 minutes to take number 9. There had been over 120 English in it. Most of the fighting had been with bayonets. When the fighting was over, the men began to dig. They were going to make the redoubts even stronger.

Robert Pincus Potts looked at the shape of Yorktown in the dark. "Can't see much," he said. "It's about 300 yards into town. Looks like we could walk in there easy."

"Don't be a fool," said Captain Wolfe. "You couldn't take 10 steps. You'd have a dozen musket balls in you. There's English soldiers every foot of the way from here to Yorktown."

Dutch had been looking around number 10. He said, "This isn't a good place for big cannon, Captain. It would be too hard to get them up here."

Potts said, "He's right, Captain. Put some 16 pounders in the trench behind us. The one we started from tonight. They can shoot down the streets of Yorktown from there. Put some coehorns—small cannon—in here. You could use them on the English between here and Yorktown."

Captain Wolfe, Potts, and Dutch went to report to Colonel Hamilton. They talked for awhile. Then Hamilton sent Wolfe, Potts, and Dutch back to report to General Lincoln.

The three worked their way back to the trench. From there they followed the road by the river. It was dark, so they could walk on the road. At last they came to the second trench. Wolfe sent Potts and Dutch back to their cannon. Then Wolfe went off to find General Lincoln.

Potts and Dutch found Captain Lamb. They told him about the fight for number 10. They told him what they had said about moving the cannons. Lamb said they had done a good night's work. Now they should find their blankets and get some sleep.

Potts and Dutch found a dry place to sleep. "Would you like to do that every night? asked Dutch.

"No, thank you," said Potts. "I'm not very brave when I'm that close to the English. Those redcoats were tough. War isn't much fun when you are face to face with a man who wants to kill you."

"I hate to think how many will die if our soldiers have to go into Yorktown," said Dutch.

The two men slept. Both had bad dreams about red bayonets chasing them.

There were no attacks the next morning. The English kept their heads down. The Americans and French went on digging new trenches. By noon, the Americans and French had about 100 cannon firing.

At dawn on October 16, Potts woke up to the sounds of muskets. He jumped to his feet and looked out of the trench. The English had attacked the French trench nearest to Yorktown.

Captain Lamb had his spyglass out. "Some of the English got into the French trench," he said. "They'll be at it with bayonets in there."

Potts' face turned white under his tan. "You ever see bayonet fighting, Captain?" he asked.

"No," said Captain Lamb.

"It ain't pretty," said Potts. "I'm glad I'm not in it."

"The English are falling back!" shouted Captain Lamb. "The French are driving them back into Yorktown."

The attack had failed. The English hadn't broken through the French lines. There were no more attacks that day. The American and French cannons went on pounding the English lines.

About midnight, the English tried a new move. They loaded soldiers into boats and rowed across the river. The soldiers were unloaded on Gloucester Point. General Cornwallis was going to take his army out of Yorktown. He hoped to break through at Gloucester. Then he would try to fight his way up to New York.

As the boats went back for a second load, a storm broke out. The waves on the river grew

high. The wind blew the little boats here and there. The boats could not make another trip. The last chance the English had was gone. They were trapped by the storm.

The cannon began roaring again on the morning of October 17. Clouds of smoke puffed out from the French and American trenches. Red dirt flew into the air as the cannonballs landed.

Then, at the far left end of the trenches, the French began to shout. They pointed at the English lines. A little drummer had climbed out of the English trench. He wore a red coat and a tall black hat. He was beating his drum.

The French cannon stopped firing. Then the Americans stopped. The drummer went on beating his drum. His drumming was calling for

a talk between officers of the two sides. An English officer climbed up by the drummer. He waved a white flag from side to side.

An American ran out from his end of the trench. He led the English officer back to the American trench. The English officer had a letter for General Washington.

An American captain took the letter. He worked his way back through the trenches. He found a horse and rode to Williamsburg. Washington was there writing to Congress and

telling them about the battle. The officer found
Washington and gave him the letter.
Washington read it. General Cornwallis wanted
to surrender his army.

There was no shooting that day or the next.
English, American, and French officers met
and worked out a plan of surrender.

At noon on October 19, the French drums
began. The French troops marched out and lined
up along the west side of the Yorktown road.
The Americans lined up across the road from the

French. People from nearby towns stood behind the soldiers.

English drums began to beat in Yorktown. English officers rode out to surrender their army. The English soldiers marched between the French and American armies. The English stacked their muskets in a meadow. Then they marched back into Yorktown. The battle was over.

Potts turned to Dutch and said, "You know what music the English band was playing? It is called *The World Turned Upside Down.* I guess that's what we did—turned their world upside down."

Epilogue

The surrender at Yorktown was not the end of the war. There was still some fighting in Ohio, South Carolina, and Georgia. King George wanted to go on fighting, but the people of England wanted the war to end.

In the spring of 1782, the English asked that all fighting be stopped. On September 3, 1783, a treaty of peace was signed. In it, the English said the United States of America had won its independence.

Yorktown, it turned out, *was* the beginning of the end for the English armies.

Potts and Dutch went home to New York. Both married and had children. Dutch's grandchildren believed his stories about the war. But Potts told so many tall tales that even his grandchildren said "Oh, Grandpa" when he told them about General Washington firing his cannon.

IMPORTANT DATES OF THE REVOLUTION

1775	April 19	Fighting at Lexington and Concord
	May 10	Ethan Allen captures Fort Ticonderoga
	June 15	George Washington elected commander-in-chief of army
	June 16/17	Battle of Bunker (Breed's) Hill;
	September	American soldiers invade Canada; Ethan Allen captured
	November/ December	British and Americans fight in Canada, South Carolina, New York, Virginia, Maine, and at sea
1776	March 17	British withdraw from Boston
	July 4	Congress adopts the Declaration of Independence
	August 27	Battle of Long Island; Americans retreat
	September 15	British take New York City
	September 16	Americans win Battle of Harlem Heights
	October 11/13	British fleet wins Battle of Lake Champlain
	October 28	British win at White Plains, N. Y.
	November 16	British take Fort Washington
	November 28	British take Rhode Island
	December	Washington takes army across Delaware and into Pennsylvania
	December 26	Washington wins Battle of Trenton, New Jersey
1777	January 3	Americans win Battle of Princeton
	January	American army winters at Morristown, New Jersey
	August 6	Battle of Oriskany, N. Y.
	August 16	Americans win Battle of Bennington, Vt.
	September 11	British win Battle of Brandywine
	September 26	British occupy Philadelphia
	October 4	British win Battle of Germantown
	October 6	British capture Forts Clinton and Montgomery
	October 7	Battles of Saratoga, N. Y.; British General Burgoyne's army surrenders October 17
	November 15	Articles of Confederation adopted
	December 18	Washington's army winters at Valley Forge

1778	February 6	France signs treaty of alliance with America
	June 18	British evacuate Philadelphia
	June 28	Americans win Battle of Monmouth Court House, N.J.
	July 4	George Rogers Clark wins at Kaskaskia
	August 29	Battle of Rhode Island; Americans retreat
	December 29	British capture Savannah, Ga.
1779	January	British take Vincennes, Ind.
	February 3	British lose at Charles Town, S. C.
	February 14	Americans win at Kettle Creek, Ga.
	February 20	Americans capture Vincennes
	March 3	British win at Briar Creek, Ga.
	June 20	Americans lose at Stono Ferry, S.C.
	July 16	Americans take Fort Stony Point, N. Y.
	August/	Fighting continues on land and sea. On September 23 John Paul Jones
	September	captures British *Serapis*
	December	Americans winter at Morristown, N.J.
1780	May 12	Charles Town surrenders to British
	June 20	Battle of Ramsour's Mills, N. C.
	July 30	Battle of Rocky Mount, S. C.
	September 26	Battle of Charlotte, N. C.
	October 7	Battle of King's Mountain, S. C.
1781	January 17	Americans win Battle of Cowpens, S. C.
	March/April	Battles in North Carolina, South Carolina, Virginia, Georgia
	October 19	British army surrenders at Yorktown
1782	July 11	British leave Savannah, Ga.
	November 30	Preliminary peace signed between America and Britain
	December 14	British leave Charleston, S. C.
1783	September 3	Final peace treaty signed
	November 25	British evacuate New York City

About the Authors:

Susan Dye Lee has been writing professionally since she graduated from college in 1961. Working with the Social Studies Curriculum Center at Northwestern University, she has created course materials in American studies. Ms. Lee has also co-authored a text on Latin America and Canada, written case studies in legal history for the Law in American Society Project, and developed a teacher's guide for tapes that explore women's role in America's past. The writer credits her students for many of her ideas. Currently, she is doing research for her history dissertation on the Women's Christian Temperance Union for Northwestern University. In her free moments, Susan Lee enjoys traveling, playing the piano, and welcoming friends to "Highland Cove," the summer cottage she and her husband, John, share.

John R. Lee enjoys a prolific career as a writer, teacher, and outdoorsman. After receiving his doctorate in social studies at Stanford, Dr. Lee came to Northwestern University's School of Education, where he advises student teachers and directs graduates in training. A versatile writer, Dr. Lee has co-authored the Scott-Foresman social studies textbooks for primary-age children. In addition, he has worked on the production of 50 films and over 100 filmstrips. His biographical film on Helen Keller received a 1970 Venice Film Festival award. His college text, *Teaching Social Studies in the Elementary School*, has recently been published. Besides pro-football, Dr. Lee's passion is his Wisconsin cottage, where he likes to shingle leaky roofs, split wood, and go sailing.

About the Artist

Michael Norman loves to draw. He has no formal training in art. Drawing since childhood, he always found art a relaxing, yet stimulating means of expression. This evolved into his present status of a free-lance artist. In addition to collecting and reading books of past and present commercial and editorial illustrators, Michael also collects comic books with one of his sons. Michael is happiest at home with his wife Anita and his four children, Eric, Mare, Michele and Cindy, who all share his interests and talent in the field of art.